Tales f the Asylum

Anecdotes from working in a Psychiatric Hospital

by

Andrew Mallett

Copyright © 2021 Andrew Mallett

ISBN: 9798473368208

All rights reserved, including the right to reproduce this book, or portions thereof in any form. No part of this text may be reproduced, transmitted, downloaded, decompiled, reverse engineered, or stored, in any form or introduced into any information storage and retrieval system, in any form or by any means, whether electronic or mechanical without the express written permission of the author.

Dedication

On 16th April 2021, our family were told the news that no family should have to hear, that our beloved Andy had been found dead at his place of work in Launceston, Tasmania.

Andy had left England in 1989 for a 'once in a lifetime trip around the world ending up in Australia', but he never returned to England to live. He fell in love with Australia and it soon became his home, eventually settling in Tasmania where he later received his Australian Citizenship and became a Justice of the Peace. Andy had a long career in Psychiatric nursing and worked in various hospitals and facilities including the Australian Red Cross, followed by his final job as a Court Liaison Officer for the Community Forensic Mental Health Service.

Andy was one of life's deep thinkers, he had a brain the size of a planet but you would never know it. Unassuming and approachable, he could relate to anyone which made him so good at his chosen profession.

As well as Psychiatric Nursing, Andy was also an expert in all things tech related and had several other websites where he advised on tech matters and wrote on a variety of other topics he was interested in, from the origins of words to his fascination with all things weird and wonderful.

Which brings us to this book.

As Andy's sisters, we felt strongly that this collection of amusing and touching stories and memories of his time as a Psychiatric Nurse that he recorded for posterity, should be preserved before they disappear into the 'celestial ether'.

So, thank you for buying this book, it was self-published by us solely out of love and in memory of Andy and as such all profits will be donated to The Red Cross.

Please enjoy the writings of our amazing big brother....

Debra & Sarah

Andrew Paul Mallett
4th December 1963 - 16th April 2021

Contents

Introduction

Mystery of the baggy trousers
A man called Horse
Commanded to Cut
Keyhole Kenny
Shock tactics
Specialling the Wrestler
Stag Night
Tripod Larry
Earning a crust
Nurses home
Student Nurse induction

Random House
Part I - Handover
Part II - Pulp friction
Part III - Student Nurses
Part IV - Initiation
Part V - Evening shift
Part VI - Rehab & Reality
Part VII - Bodily fluids

Psychosurgery
I see dead people…everywhere
Gallows Humour

Andrew Mallett - A potted history

Introduction

The history of Psychiatric care is one which is distinguished by stories of both heroism and cruelty. Attitudes to mental illness and treatment have been as much subject to the whims of politics, science, religion and fashion as any other aspects of human behaviour.

We now live in a time where attitudes to severe psychological disorders are much more tolerant than they have been in times gone by. In the past, such people might have been deemed to be 'possessed' by evil spirits or even just 'bad' people. Nowadays, certainly in the Western world we tend to use a sickness/health model to provide a framework from which to view what is happening.

The Medical Model seeks to classify, collate, study and treat mental disorders as if they were the same as pathological physical conditions. People are treated in hospitals, clinics and health centres and encouraged to lead as normal a life as possible, preferably in the community rather than in large institutions.

Despite this, the old attitudes can tend to linger somewhat. Although many of the erstwhile Asylums - the big psychiatric hospitals of the last couple of centuries - have closed down or changed their roles, the stigma and the stories still live on.

I hope you will enjoy these stories. I have been fortunate enough to have worked with so many interesting people over the years. A large number of them have left me deeply moved and will never be forgotten. Certain details have been changed out of respect and to protect confidentiality.

Andy

Mystery of the Baggy Trousers

My first training placement was on a male 'long-stay' ward. There were approximately 30 patients, most of whom had been living in the hospital for most of their lives. The average age was around 50. I looked up one chap's case notes. He was 61 years old and had been admitted to the hospital at the age of 18 for stealing some items from a local shop. Oh, and he had epilepsy. He'd been living in the institution ever since. Sadly, such cases were not unusual.

I liked the patients on the ward and enjoyed playing pool, going for walks and generally interacting with them. The blokes were used to the regular rotation of students around the place and tolerated the new faces well. After a few days I was beginning to feel like a Real Psychiatric Nurse and was glad I'd given up my bank job. This was the life for me.

I kept noticing one of the old blokes who hobbled around with a walking frame (known as a Zimmer frame) and a pained look on his face. Arthur took absolutely ages to get from A to B and would've put the average snail to shame. He also had the baggiest pair of trousers imaginable. "Fair enough," I thought. Ward 13 was not what you'd consider a mecca of fashion. In fact, the standard issue pair of male 'institution trousers', which usually ended about six inches up the leg, was a constant source of bemusement to all who beheld them.

Arthur didn't speak very much and indeed, didn't seem to do much of anything really, preferring to rest in 'his' chair and watch the telly. It's a feature of institutionalised behaviour - some of the patients had been using the same seat for years and could get quite stroppy if you were to unwittingly sit in 'their' chair. Come to think of it, I know a few other people who are a bit like that too...

So as the days went by, I would watch Arthur's painstaking to-ing and fro-ing, his large trousers a continuing source of intrigue. I amused myself imagining them flapping in the breeze as he shot down the hallway on a jet powered Zimmer. Then one day Ian the charge nurse, asked me to take Arthur for a bath.

It's a general principle of rehabilitation that one gets the individual to do as much as they can for themselves, but Arthur was clearly not going anywhere in a hurry, as it were, and needed a fair bit of help to undress and bathe himself. It was at this point that the mystery of the baggy trousers unfurled itself before my very eyes. Local witnesses (including a smirk-ridden Ian) later claimed they heard my squeak from a good hundred paces away, but as Arthur dropped his strides, there before me appeared the largest scrotum I'd ever set eyes on. I mean, I didn't think I'd led that sheltered a life, but Arthurs gonad's would've made an elephant blush.

Turns out the poor bugger had an inoperable scrotal hernia. Otherwise known as an inguinal hernia, this is where part of the abdominal wall can become weakened, allowing some of the intestinal organs to protrude into the groin area.

Arthur's hernia was inoperable because he was a 79-year-old 'psychiatric patient' who wasn't in the best of health and was unlikely to make it into surgery. His balls were so big they almost touched his knee and his penis had all but disappeared from the massive stretching of flesh. Helping him to wash was a true lesson in sponging-softly. To my surprise though, he seemed pretty relaxed about the whole thing, he just didn't move fast.

Suddenly Arthur's demeanour and generosity of trouser made a whole lot of sense and I gained a whole new respect for the poor fellow. I've also been very careful about how I lift heavy things ever since.

A MAN CALLED HORSE

A modern trend is for the old Mental Health Institutions of the past to be closed down and for people to be treated on psychiatric wards placed within general hospitals. I thought I'd seen everything until one day, when a man was admitted to the psych unit I was working on.

You see some bizarre sights in this business, but a man dressed as a theatrical horse standing in the corridor, believing in all seriousness that he was a real horse, is not something which occurs every day.

Schizophrenia hits about one per cent of the world population, irrespective of race, religion, ethnicity, etc. It's about as common as diabetes. In a similar way that knowing someone has cancer tells you very little about their actual condition, schizophrenia can be many different things to many different sufferers. Diagnosis is made from a wide range of possible symptoms, experienced over a specific time period.

It was helpful that our man responded verbally during most of our conversations with him, as none of us was well versed in *Equestrian*. However, the intermittent horsey neighs and snorts certainly provided an interesting spectacle and a good reason to keep a handy box of tissues nearby.

It was fortunate to the humour of the situation that our man was 'happily mad'. He didn't seem particularly disturbed by his condition and despite his convictions, often quipped around the place good-humouredly. Although he appeared at times to believe he was a real horse, he seemed to realise the humour of the situation. We did wonder if he was having a lend of us for a while.

One common feature of psychotic conditions including schizophrenia, is delusions. A delusion is a fixed belief which a person holds, despite evidence to the contrary, which is out of keeping with their usual socio-religious and cultural background.

So, if a priest says he is able to converse directly with God, then it would probably be deemed a claim which is appropriate to his standing. Whereas if a true blue fourth generation Aussie bloke claims he is a reincarnation of a German officer of the Third Reich and refuses to acknowledge the authority of the police, to the point of threatening the cops with a knife (another past client of mine), then you'd probably be fairly safe in saying this chap was somewhat deluded and his resultant behaviour deemed it necessary that he receives treatment before he or someone else gets seriously hurt (they shot him in the arm)...

Of course, as is typical of psychiatry, many situations are rarely cut-and-dried. There are often many 'shades of grey' and options for Assessment Team debate, relating to when 'normality' (whatever that is) begins, eccentricity takes over and insanity is certain. But it *is* relatively easy when you've got a man in equestrian attire (and I'm not talking jodhpurs here) with a horse's head, neighing like the best of them, to come to a conclusion that this is not a real horse, just a man dressed up. Unfortunately, convincing the chap himself that this was the case, was a lot harder.

On another notable occasion the catering department were somewhat bemused at the requested special dietary requirements, but this just turned out to be a bit of a joke on behalf of one of the black-humoured RNs and 'Mr. Ed' was actually happy to partake of a normal human diet, with the standard knife and fork routine (no nosebags for *him*).

In treating people with such conditions, it is unwise to confront an individual's delusional material directly, as this can often lead to behavioural aggravation and a breaking down of the trust you are trying to develop. However, neither can you agree with what they say, as this may promote a reinforcing of their beliefs and an untherapeutic 'collusive' relationship.

People with delusional thoughts are often totally convinced of the reality of their convictions, however bizarre; as convinced as you are that you are a member of the human race and living on the planet Earth. Prevailing treatment consists of careful doses of antipsychotic medication and cautious, reality reinforcing therapeutic relationships, where the individual is gently introduced to the other realities that most of the rest of us share.... most of the time.

As it turned out, our man responded quite quickly to the antipsychotic medication and left the clinic a new man. We never heard from him again and I often wonder what he's doing now (joined a circus?) and how he looks back on this time in his life.

COMMANDED TO CUT

People with psychotic illnesses such as Schizophrenia often experience a wide range of symptoms. One common set of features are hallucinations: false perceptions with no external stimulus. These can affect any sense such as sight, hearing, touch, taste and smell as well as the perception of one's own body.

Typically, a person with Schizophrenia may report auditory hallucinations - hearing voices for which there is no external evidence. These voices, which seem as real as any spoken words, may be of someone familiar or unfamiliar, perhaps even one's own voice perceived as if spoken aloud. The voices are often reported as unpleasant, commonly making derogatory remarks about the individual themselves or commenting on the sufferer's actions.

One disturbing subset of this phenomena are command hallucinations. The voices tell the individual to do something, often leading to erratic and extremely unpredictable behaviour. The commands can be so compelling that those experiencing them feel unable to resist. Such unpredictability can make it very hard to look after these people.

In milder (although still extremely debilitating) cases, the instructions might be to walk up and down a room five hundred times or to touch something. In more severe examples the sufferer might find themselves compelled to behave more destructively. It was an example of the latter that caused an event of the bloodiest violence.

Steven, a slim quiet-spoken fellow in his early twenties, had been on the ward for three weeks when it happened. He had recently been diagnosed with Schizophrenia and spent most of his time quietly reading or watching the television. On this particular afternoon, Steven had taken himself into the bathroom for a bit of a dip. Although the staff knew he heard disturbing voices, he was responding to treatment and there was certainly no reason to suspect what he was capable of doing.

So, it was perhaps by chance that one of the Staff Nurses walked into the bathroom and spotted the blood dripping down the walls of the cubicle. The security alarm was raised and the cubicle door smashed-in. In no time flat nurses were running in from all directions. There in the bath lay Steven, the blood pumping across the room from his wrists, where his left hand was hanging from the bone. Apparently unaware of any pain, he was desperately trying to cut his other hand off with the razor blade held in his mouth.

As a nurse, it's in emergency situations like this that your mind becomes extremely focussed. No time to think. Just time to do. With the years of training and experience to fall back on, you know what needs to be done. Only later will you reflect on the horror of what you've just been through. Stop the bleeding. Try not to skid on the slippery floor. Blood everywhere. Elevate the limb. Apply a compressed bandage - the towels. Keep the breathing. Keep the heart beating. Get the water out of the bath. Get him out of the bath. On the floor. Keep him warm. Blankets. Alert emergency services. First Aid trolley. Drugs. Oxygen. Defibrillator.

IV fluids. How much blood loss before he goes into shock? Will he survive? What about his hand?

Events of such bloody extremes are thankfully relatively uncommon, although inpatient Psychiatric Units by their nature are places where angst and despair are often played out, behind closed doors, away from society. It can certainly put everyday life into a different perspective. Things which seem to shock others, outside the walls can seem pretty mundane in comparison.

The surgeons managed to save Steven's almost amputated hand, although it's hard to say if he will ever regain full use of it. The treatment and physiotherapy continue. He said the voices told him to do it. He said he felt no pain. And now when Steven looks down at the contracted claw which was once his right hand, he will always be reminded of the day the voices told him he was disgusting and should never be able to touch himself, or anyone else again.

KEYHOLE KENNY

Often when I was updating the medical notes on the long-stay wards, I would look back to see the circumstances surrounding the patient's original admission. A sad fact of the times is that many of the people on the wards had been there for most of their lives.

In the bad old days up to the mid-20th Century, people were sometimes locked up for the merest peccadillo such as stealing a loaf of bread and often remained there until they died. The British had a great system of dealing with their undesirables through a system of removal: 'criminals' got transportation to the Australian colonies and the 'insane' got locked away in the asylums, often some distance from the major towns.

One such fellow was Kenny. An inpatient from his teens, he was now in his mid-fifties; a tall, thin, wiry man with a sharp beak of a nose and wild, staring eyes. He had originally been removed from his house for stealing from the neighbours.

However, because of his slightly odd demeanour and the fact that he claimed to hear voices telling him to do stuff, Kenny was incarcerated in the local bin which just happened to be a couple of miles up the road from his house. As time went on, Kenny had gotten sicker and his place was eventually sold and the money put in a trust fund for him.

Poor Kenny never could completely come to terms with being in hospital and across the decades, his mental state varied like that of his peers. He had a bit of a short fuse at times and it wasn't unusual for Ken to get into fights with other patients on the ward. During periods of extreme psychosis, Kenny would sometimes abscond from the ward and run off down the road.

Onlookers would watch in shock as Kenny fanged down the main street at full pelt, hair streaming, institution trousers riding up his calves and a mad look in his eye. Close behind would (usually) be a couple of male RNs, white coats streaming in the breeze, pelting along in hot pursuit. People knew the hospital and knew what it was for and it sort of helped to keep up appearances every once in a while. Good training for the nurses too.

The real problem was when we didn't notice that he'd slipped away. Given the time and the opportunity, Kenny would occasionally actually return to his old house and knock on the door and insist on being allowed back into 'his' place. When the owner refused, Ken would usually resort to some minor form of violence such as punching out the owner.

It wasn't unusual for the hospital to get a call from the distraught householder, saying that Kenny was bashing on his front door or trying to poke things through the keyhole and could we come and please pick him up. The last time I looked I think the count stood at seven for the number of tenants who had vacated the place somewhat hurriedly, after sustaining broken noses and cut lips from one of Kenny's 'house calls'.

Shock Tactics

"Keep his arm still, he's spitting it out!"
I held the 72-year-old man's arm harder against his mattress, the other three nurses firming their grip on his other three limbs, as the Senior Staff Nurse pushed the tube into his mouth.

Bertie spluttered and coughed as Ken, the senior nurse carefully syringed the formula down his throat, while trying not to let him aspirate on the stuff.

"Fuck, I did not sign up for this..." I struggled to hold back my own bile as I watched Ken's muscular arm covering the old man's mouth, preventing him from spitting it out. It was like something from a twisted and tragically one-sided wrestling match. The other nurses shifted uneasily and tried to offer words of encouragement to the stricken old man.

Ken spoke his own words of encouragement and comfort to the frail skeleton of a figure helpless in his lap. Incongruous with his stranglehold-like demeanour, he also picked up on the group's discomfiture...

"We had Bertie here two years ago, didn't we Bert. Last time he'd managed to lose nearly 4 stone (25KG) and couldn't even get out of bed. His son and daughter were beside themselves."

Bert gargled and thrashed as he desperately tried to expel the liquid which was helping him to stay alive.

Ken continued, partly to try and reassure Bertie, partly for the benefit of the senior students (and junior staffs) for whom this kind of treatment seemed to go completely against anything they'd ever encountered in their short careers.

"We tried coaxing and persuasion, Ken's son and daughter pleaded with him. But he said nothing and ate or drank nothing. Just sat and stared at the wall. He pulled out the drips so there was no point in trying NG tubes. And now his weight's dropped so low that unless he takes in some nourishment, he's likely to go into organ failure."

"So how long do we have to go on like this?" asked Andy.

"Until tonight. Tomorrow Bert's scheduled for ECT. It's the only thing that seems to work for him."

Andy nodded. Not a great fan of modified electroconvulsive therapy, he had nevertheless seen it make a difference for some patients. Some people considered it a slightly controversial treatment, partly because in the past it had been used indiscriminately, overused for all sorts of diagnoses. Andy remembered reading it had even been used as a form of behaviour modification or punishment.

These days, treatment was usually given as a last resort, after counselling and medications had been tried. Except in emergencies, the patient's consent was required, after a full explanation of the procedure and possible side effects. The 'modified' bit meant patients were given a pre-med, muscle relaxants and a full but short-lasting general anaesthetic. The electrodes placed against the temples transferred a minute current, just enough to produce a generalised seizure, lasting about 10 seconds.

If it worked, the results were almost instantaneous. A few more treatments plus adjunctive pharmacotherapy often saw the patient leaving with a marked improvement. But to this day I've never seen an improvement from ECT like I did in dear Bertie.

On admission he would sit in his chair and stare at the wall. Totally mute. He would do nothing for himself, acknowledge no-one and he actively, physically resisted any attempts to help him. He even defecated where he sat. This was one of the most profoundly depressed people I had ever seen. And the physical assaults on the poor man to ensure he got nourishment was also taking its toll on the staff morale.

Other patients too were aware of the old man in the side room who just stared at the walls. They saw the doors close behind the nurses who went into his room and were surely aware of the existential struggle going on within.

After just one ECT session, Bertie started to eat food and shower. After two ECT sessions he was smartly dressed, clean shaven and digging into his hospital food. We started to see his true character. Bertie would walk around the ward, sharing jokes with others, sticking his head into the Nurses Station to pass a wry comment, popping out for a puff on a cigarette as he walked with his son and daughter around the hospital grounds.

It was a total transformation in which the whole ward, patients and staff revelled; it seemed to bring everybody closer in a collective, reflective hope for our futures. It was almost as sad when Bertie left with his grateful son and daughter as when he'd arrived and the whole ward community waved him off.

Specialling the Wrestler

Fact: It's very hard to stop someone from killing themselves if they're really determined enough. However, on this occasion, this was my primary objective.

In psych nursing circles, protecting someone from harming themselves in hospital is called 'specialling'. It is total one-to-one care. It's a huge responsibility and a great drain on one's nervous system (not to mention staffing resources). It's also not really great for the patient, who has to forego all privacy and personal space privileges, including having escorted toilet trips.

The person is usually kept in a safe room away from the main ward area, where they may spend up to several weeks eating and sleeping and passing the time with the special nurses and perhaps the occasional visitor, until the depression lifts. Not ideal, but certainly better than ending your life prematurely and often violently. With the right care and treatment, most actively suicidal people eventually decide to carry on living once they start feeling better within themselves.

Big Kev had been admitted to the Acute Psych Unit after slashing both his wrists with a razor blade. He was extremely depressed and had made quite a mess of his arms in the process of cutting them, as you do. Both arms were heavily sutured (stitched) and bandaged up to the elbows. Big Kev looked like he'd got a long pair of sweatbands on his huge, chunky forearms - a bit like you see those all-in wrestlers wearing in the ring. Which is quite fitting really, because Big Kev was an all-in wrestler.

It was Kev's second major episode of depression and he'd been started on the usual course of antidepressants and mild sedatives to make his days a bit more bearable. He'd been on the ward for about two weeks and because of his admitted suicidality (not everyone owns up), was being specialled in a side room. His arms were in such a mess that a plastics consult had been sought and Kev needed to be transferred temporarily to one of the general hospitals for some surgery.

This is where I first met Big Kev in person. He wasn't originally an inpatient from my own unit's catchment area, but as one of the nurses in the department with a fair bit of specialling experience, I'd agreed to help out. I'd read up on his case file and been briefed about the situation, which was a slightly unusual one - specialling someone away from the comfort zone of the specialist psychiatric units. But I like a challenge and a challenge is just what I got.

After taking the handover from the departing nurse as they went off duty, there I was. Just me and this big bloke, closed up in a small side room together for the next 8 hours. Physically he was about as big as I'd expected (5'11" - about an inch taller than me; 260 pounds - over 100lbs heavier than me!) and he had a bit of a fierce look about him, sitting there with his wild hair, stubbly chin and hospital issue dressing gown and I remember thinking:

a) I'm glad I'm not standing in a ring on the opposite side from this bloke right now
b) No. I'm just shut up all alone in a room with him
c) Ah, but he's the one he wants to hurt...

Not that the two of us would be sitting here like this if there'd been any question of psychosis or any risk of danger to others. He'd been here a day already; surgery was scheduled for tomorrow morning and he'd be back on the unit again soon enough. Although not soon enough for Kev.

We talked for a while and during this time I performed an MSE (mental state examination) to assess, amongst other things, Kev's state of suicidality. What he said caused me some concern, because he said he was feeling a bit more energetic and denied any suicidal feelings or intentions. I knew from the nursing report that the day before, he'd still been pretty low and on the edge.

Either Kev was lying to me and he actually did have a plan (people can 'perk up' when they know it's all going to be over soon) or he was indeed feeling a bit better (in psychiatry a recognised danger zone: a depressed and amotivational person, too low to even kill themselves, may actually act on suicidal impulses once they start to get their energy back). Either way, I wasn't happy and Kev was starting to pace.

You know, the way a lion does, up and down its cage.

Now, after a couple of hours I'd had a little time to build up some rapport with Kev but as time passed, both his patience and my conversational repertoire were starting to get a bit stretched. The extra medication I'd given him to promote relaxation didn't seem to be doing much good, probably in large part to his Neanderthal constitution. He requested a walk to help him burn off some energy and, after a moment contemplating the consequences of a refusal (Headline: "Nurse's body found stuffed in laundry bag")(again) agreed, on the proviso that we keep strictly within the hospital grounds.

The walk brought a much-needed reduction in Big Kev's level of arousal (and for a few precious moments, mine too) and we strolled like a couple of lifelong chums. And one of those lives was rapidly ticking towards an untimely end.

One of the principles of specialling is that you keep the person within arm's reach - so you can grab them if they do something desperate. I still think back now to what might have happened if I'd actually managed to keep hold of Big Kev's arm. One minute he was beside me, the next he was head down and running at full pelt. I was nearly pulled off my feet and, like in some surreal funny/terrifying scenario, I imagine I must have looked like some cartoon character flailing along horizontal-fashion behind some maddened bull, hurtling out of control towards the busy road.

What followed reminded me of that scene in the film 'An American Werewolf in London', where the werewolf breaks loose in the middle of the Metropolis and the incredible chaos which ensues. I still have the image of that scene burned into my mind.

As I ran after him, Kev reached the main street and kept running, straight into the busy lunchtime traffic, straight into the path of a double-decker bus. It hit him at full speed, square on. There was an incredible bang, Kev was flipped spreadeagled about 20ft up into the air and came crashing down on his back. The bus driver reacted quickly and as he brought the huge bus to a dead stop, the successive skids and crashes of the traffic stoving into the back of the bus could be heard. A car coming in the opposite direction slammed on the brakes, was smashed in the back by two other cars and came to a skidding stop with its wheels pinning down Kev's dressing gown. Women were screaming, a pedestrian fainted, nurses and staff came running out of the hospital. It was utter chaos.

As I reached Kev, I could see he was still conscious and breathing. I told him not to move. As I covered him with a blanket, he just looked up at me and said, "Sorry Andy...."

The ambulances seemed to take an eternity arrive (one for m'man, one for the pedestrian). Somebody started directing the traffic. I sat on the road with Kev. I looked at him lying there. I looked around at the carnage surrounding us. I yelled at a couple of unfortunate do-gooders who wanted to transfer Kev tidily onto the pavement so the traffic could get going again (good tension release there). The police arrived and started sorting out the mess. I got the hospital administrator to contact the ward and the psych unit to let them know what had happened. Then it was into the back of the ambulance with a still-conscious Kev and away, weaving through the trail of smashed vehicles and astonished onlookers.

Kev was given an initial once over in casualty and seemed to be in not too bad a shape considering. You soon know when you're at the bottom of the triage food chain. The X-Rays took ages.

Explaining the administrative situation was interesting, "Yes well Kev is actually a registered inpatient in two hospitals in this Health Authority at the moment, three if you include here..." etc. I really thought I was gonna get my arse kicked over this one ("You let him do what!!?"), but my boss was actually quite fine about it and showed great concern over my own well-being.

The X-Rays showed no breakages. In fact, Kev had come through the whole experience without a scratch (I hear the pedestrian got a fairly severe concussion).

As we strolled out of Casualty that evening to take the ambulance transport back, Kev looked at me and said, "Never again." He was a man of few words.

Stag Night

Generally speaking, nurses have a bit of a rep for working hard, but they are equally fond of playing hard too, especially Psych nurses. 'If you can't get a girlfriend, get a nurse' as the saying goes. The stresses of the job and the uniqueness of the situations which they find themselves in behind the closed doors of the wards, make for an interesting perspective on life.

Of course, psychiatric nursing in particular takes the bizarre to new heights of normality. I suppose when insanity, violence and tragedy are the norm of one's working environment, then this eventually becomes the baseline for 'normality' and thus new heights of weirdness need to be sought out, just to get your kicks. It is with this background that I ruefully recount the following anecdote...

Now, when a chum or colleague (esp. male) is getting married, it's often considered the right thing to play some little trick on them, just to show how much you care. Typical scenarios include taking them out with the boys (and girls) and getting them so pissed that they don't turn up in time (if at all) for the marriage ceremony. Other jolly prenuptial japes include escorting them to a strip joint for a night of inebriated sleaze ("Well it's yer last night of freedom mate"), shoving a tub of axle grease down their pubes (garage mechanics take note), sticking them on a train to Glasgow or indeed, all three.

Dave was a popular senior nurse on our psychiatric unit. A quiet, unassuming fellow of gentle demeanour, Dave was a bit of a hippy to be sure, distinguished by his dry wit and wry perspectives on life. And he was getting married tomorrow...

I'm sure the idea was just to chuck him in the bath - an inductive privilege usually reserved for fledgling student nurses - or give him a traditional moistening with the fire hose. But, well I suppose the sense of occasion went to everybody's head and before anyone knew what was happening, Dave had been dragged outside by several staff members, stripped naked, tied to a tree, had a bottle of ink squirted over his privates and was being hosed down with a fire hose so powerful that it took two staff members to hold it on target. Honestly, the poor bugger looked like some bedraggled and forlorn Jesus figure. It was a bit surreal really.

I must say that he took it quite well and (eventually) managed to see the funny side. Something which can't be said for the hospital Administrator who called the ward the next day, demanding an explanation. I managed to convince him that it had all been my own idea. Perhaps my colleagues had all been under some sort of Machiavellian influence. The boss acknowledged the tradition of the situation but suggested a more low-key approach which didn't include semi-crucifixion and hydraulic torture, in future.

Apparently, it took five weeks for all the ink to come off...

Tripod Larry

One thing you could say about the old institutions: they contained some real characters. One man who particularly stands out in my memory was Larry. A resident on one of the long stay wards for many years, Larry like many others suffered from schizophrenia. In a similar pattern to his peers, Larry was over the acute phase of the illness and rarely suffered from severe 'attacks' of psychosis any more.

It was a psychotic episode a few years earlier however, that had left Larry wheelchair bound and provided me with one of the most disturbing sights of my career. It had been one of England's coldest winters and Larry had been out for one of his regular long walks in the hospital grounds. The gardens of many of the big old psychiatric hospitals were often stunning, managed as they were by teams of resident inpatients who maintained the horticultural beauty as part of their occupational therapy. I love walking through the grounds of these old hospitals and imagining all the stories. I think it was a great shame when such tending was deemed to be 'exploitation' and the job was handed over to professional gardeners, often leaving the hospital residents with very little to do.

Being a man of habit, Larry was usually back from his walks for the evening meal, but as tea time came and went, concern mounted and a search was made of the grounds and surrounding area. Unfortunately, it gets dark early on the cold winter evenings and our man was nowhere to be found. It was decided that another search be carried out at first light.

The following morning Larry was found face down in a hedge on a perimeter of the hospital, his legs literally dangling in the air. The initial relief in finding him and the comical nature of his predicament were soon replaced with a deeper concern. Considering he'd just spent the night out in the open he was in a bit of a bad shape. The hedge had protected him a little but his legs were badly frost-bitten. No-one could really figure out how he'd got stuck in the hedge, but he was floridly psychotic, talking to hallucinatory voices and unable to recognise any familiar faces.

As it turned out nothing could be done to save Larry's legs and he had to have a bi-lateral below the knee amputation. Although he seemed to adjust to his wheelchair-bound life admirably, Larry never spoke again and would only communicate in grunts and murmurs.

One of the worst things I have ever seen was during a subsequent psychotic episode, years later. He had been unwell for a couple of days, muttering under his breath and staring at the walls. We were all sitting in the lounge one evening after supper when Larry literally jumped out of his wheelchair and ran screaming across the floor *on his stumps*. We managed to catch up with him and were able to treat his psychosis which soon abated once more, but his legs took months of dressings to heal and must have caused him some shocking pain. But he never complained or winced once.

His nickname? Well amongst his other qualities, as you've probably guessed Larry was rather well endowed...

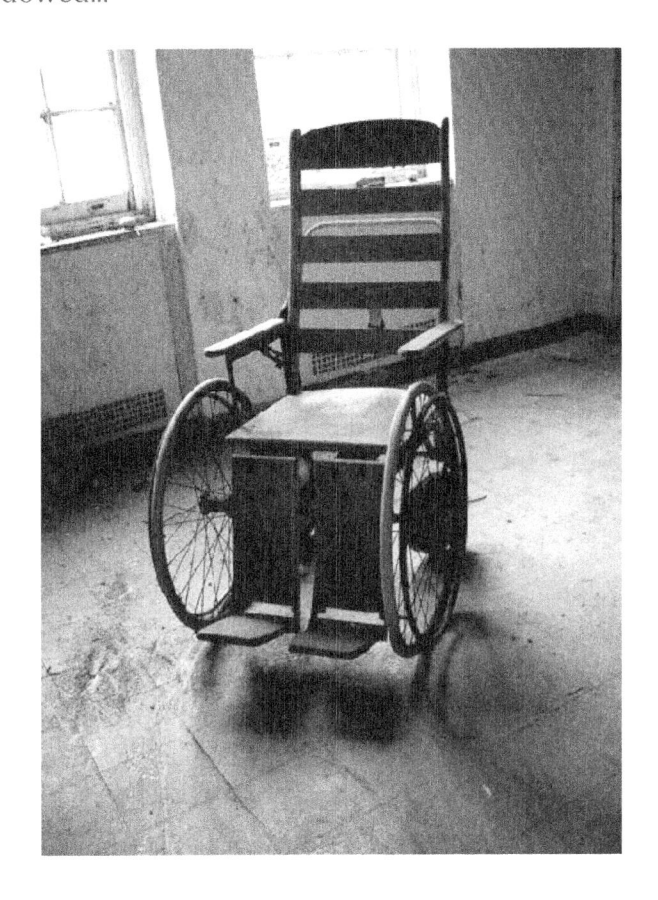

Earning a crust..

"I need to take a look inside your vagina..."
Sometimes you've just gotta say what you mean and Enrolled Nurse Bridget Hargreves wasn't beating about the bush (yet) as she attempted to escort patient June Southerby to the ladies' block, while at the same time efficiently wiping June's cheek with a kleenex. It was a regular ritual that neither enjoyed but Bridget (being the only female on-duty) tackled the task with her usual aplomb. But the woman riled;

"No f*ck off! You're not comin' near my ~~snatch~~ you l#sbian b*tch!"
June enjoyed a forthright manner of communicating and was good at expressing how she felt, without the need for superfluous small talk.

However, the eloquent June was no match for the seasoned expertise of EN Hargreves, who knew her job as well as anyone who had spent the last 20 years working the 'bins'. Bridget slipped the packet of Dunhill Red into her nurse's tunic pocket with a practised flourish which was at once both ostentatious and clandestine (and an absolute pleasure to behold for the observing male nurses). The couple meandered towards the female cubicles.

Ian the Charge Nurse - never one to miss a didactic opportunity - peered over his coffee mug towards the fledgling greenhorn in the corner...

"Now that, Young Andy, is what we call 'persuasion'..."

The nursing student nodded in reverence. Three months into his training, *Young Andy* was diligent in the assimilation of all aspects of **The Craft**. In fact, he was so keen he would have gladly performed the *PV* examination himself, but this was '*...not strictly necessary at the moment, lad...*' Andy's restless, latex-clad digits would be restricted to the clinical exploration of the male rectum for the time being.

"So why does June need to be examined?" asked Andy.

Ian met his student's gaze; was the boy ready for the brutal realities of asylum life? Well, Andy had dealt with getting Old Kenny up the other morning and helping the man to shower off the remains of the night's vomit, which had solidified into a kind of nocturnally-harvested crusty tube arrangement from mouth to pillow. Ian made a decision: Andy was ready.

The charge nurse continued, "Every pay day, June goes out to the hospital grounds to visit the male patients in the gardening group. There she 'services' them in exchange for a few quid and stores the pound notes in her 'purse'. Today is pay-day."

Ian went on to explain that much effort had been put into preventing this unusual behaviour over the years, but June - who suffers from Chronic Schizophrenia - had always found ways to return to her remunerative activities when left to her own devices. The main issue was considered to be June's health in terms of prompt removal of said monies from the *cha-cha* to prevent putrefaction and infection.

The only serious victim of this state of affairs had suffered during the early days of June's innocent routine. One Mr. Malcolm Tibbis ("Moneybags Mal"), owner of the hospital tuck shop had experienced a near myocardial infarction after June had approached his kiosk with the intention of procuring cigarettes with some of her recently-earned (and still warm) cash.

"And to think I gave up working in a bank to come here... I'll never look at a pound note the same again," mused Andy.

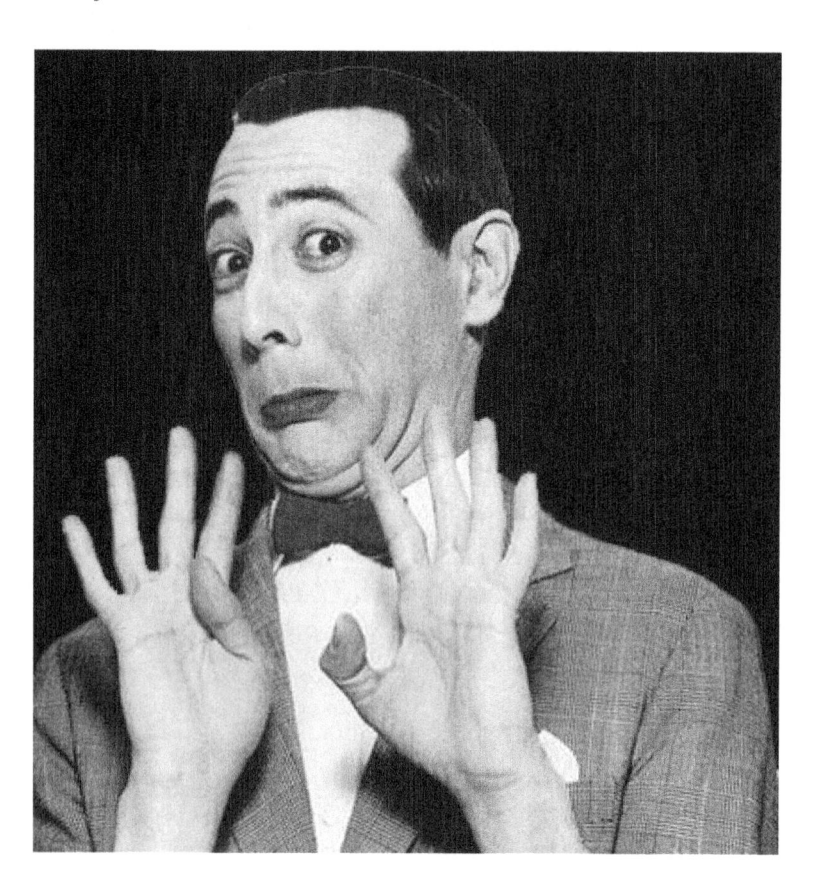

Nurses Home

Back in the day, every self-respecting hospital had a nurses' home. A safe place for the dear hearts to live while they were working hard on the wards. It was originally a somewhat cloistered life with a resident warden/matron who would keep an eye on things and maintain decorum and curfews and provide support.

Well, that was the theory.

Imagine then rooms full of young ladies, most subject to the hormonal excesses of youth, many away from home for the first time. I think the warden had her work cut out...

As time went on, nursing became less religiously influenced and things gradually got a little.... looser. As the curfews started to disappear, the hushed stories of climbing in and out of the ground floor window belonging to the 'gate nurse' started to fade.

Enter the Eighties and although things were much more relaxed, there was still Much Fun To Be Had. Especially when males began taking up the profession and also started 'living in'.

Our Nurses' Home was called <u>Drayton Old Lodge</u> a 1914 manor house with an ancient 15th Century monument looming in the grounds. And it was awesome. There was the original part, looking all grand and austere (containing the best rooms) and a more modern wing with dozens of smaller bedsit rooms. To get a better room, you had to wait for someone to move out and then work your way up. The grandest rooms were inhabited by three Philippino nurses who had come over in the 70s and definitely weren't budging! I didn't blame them...

Working in the psychiatric hospitals had its quirks and stresses so as we worked hard, we also played verily. Room 'visits' were *de rigueur* and corridor parties cheered us as much as they infuriated hospital administration (something about extra vacuuming, empty bottles and candle wax in the carpet). If you wanted to socialise there was always someone around or you could just stay in your room and blast out some music.
Of the numerous jolly japes which routinely occurred, some honourable mentions come to mind. One hot Summer's day spurned a spontaneous water pistol fight, starting inside, moving outside. Weaponry gradually escalated (as things tend to do with a bit of alcohol on board) from hand-squirters (!) to Fairy Liquid bottles to my own customised M16 water gun, modified to carry two extra tanks of detergent bottles. Thought I'd won that one until the firehose came out...

One year we organised a mediaeval fayre for Lodge residents and serfs. Ancient attire was the go. The games were a variation on a theme. The opening blindfolded three-legged egg-and-spoon race went down well, as did the contestants. A sideshow of stocks and wet sponges provided ongoing punishments for various misdemeanours (real or invented).

I made up a couple of papier-mache horses' heads. Two helmets (made from buckets and foam) were fashioned, with suction cups from a couple of sink-plungers screwed to the tops. Two 'knights' piggy-backed and guided the horse people (who couldn't see out) and had to try to knock a ball from the suction cup on top of the opposing warrior's helmet, using makeshift 'morning stars' (the sink plunger handles with rope and a ball on the end). I don't know what hurt more, our aching sides or the heads of the competitors - probably should've used a bit more foam inside them buckets.

The final contest involved two teams seated opposite along a lengthy table. Blindfolded, they had to feed the person opposite a bright green porridge using very long spoons. The light was fading (no electricity in the Middle Ages) so my mate Ady brought out his XJ750 which offered an eerie headlight glow to the proceedings. I can still see in my mind's eye the utter mayhem as globs of luminous porridge flew in and out of focus across the gloom in the ensuing food fight. I could barely catch my breath for laughing.

Student Nurse Inductions

Psychiatry can be a very high-stress occupation and I tend to think that the innovative ways which people find for relieving that stress often reflect such extremes. Like many professions, Psych nursing has its great traditions and this is certainly true for some of the treatments specially reserved for the benefit and edification of the fledgling student nurse.

After a twelve-week placement on Ward 13, I was still reeling a bit from 'Scrotum-Shock' (technical term), but I think otherwise I'd got off pretty lightly. Little did I know what my next placement held in store: Psychogeriatrics.

The Charge Nurse of this ward for the elderly and infirm of mind, was a fantastic bloke. Ivan was a BIG fellow who was big on patient care and big on student training. His right-hand man Mike, closely resembled Ivan in his all-in-wrestler physique and his enthusiasm for making guests welcome. So, I suppose it was to no surprise that the end of my first week on the ward found me swarthily bundled into a hospital linen bag and dangling out of a window, with my boots hanging from a nearby tree.

Psychogeriatric care is by its nature, a somewhat messy business. Incontinence - both urinary and faecal - are unfortunate facts of life (and that was just the staff) as our elderly folk gradually lost their grip on life and bodily wastes. It was often a sad sight to behold, but

Ivan's team did their utmost to offer the best quality of life under the circumstances. And plenty of entertainment.

On one occasion I arrived early on the ward, full of enthusiasm after a fine weekend away (the roster gave you one long weekend every 6 weeks). As I donned my protective hospital standard-issue white coat I found that someone had sewn it up at the wrists. Popping the stitching provided only momentary triumph as my hands disappeared into deep pockets filled with talcum powder and something resembling KY Jelly.

Looking back, I'm not sure what I miss more, the impromptu fully clothed bath-attacks, the enema fights, the strapped-tightly-in-the-wheelchair death rides, or perhaps it was the old 'dip your finger in the bedpan and lick it afterward like I just did' routine. A sharp learner soon learnt to adopt the subtle change-of-finger technique.

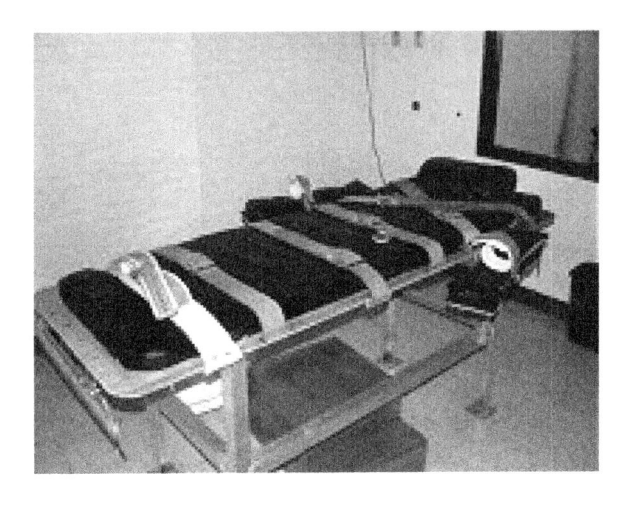

Random

House

Part I: Handover..

You always know when you've arrived for duty at **Random House**. *If the acrid stench of stale piss doesn't get you first, then the low, almost subliminal murmur of hushed voices interspersed with the occasional cackle of maniacal laughter will. And that's just coming out of the staff room...*

Andy kicked open the door to the nurses' station - standard procedure - and went to chuck his backpack down on the chair which wasn't covered with skid marks. However, as such chairs do not actually exist at *Random*, he plopped his bag down on the floor as usual and decided to stand for a while. The day shift was handing over the day's activities to the night shift.

Almost as one, the gathered throng turned briefly to nod a welcome, then the collective (un)consciousness was returned to Maudlin, the nurse in charge of that day's shift. As usual, people were doing their best to stifle yawns as the monotonous drone continued. But if their slightly watery eyes gave them away, Maudlin appeared not to notice.

"Brian had quite a good day today. He got up for breakfast and had a shave and a shower and passed a good bowel motion..." (*'But not all at once I hope,'* Andy thought to himself)

"And Grezelda had a good day too..." (*'Yeah, well if you consider getting out of bed, staring at a dry face-washer for 20 minutes, smoking 50 cigarettes and shitting your pants, a good day,'* Andy mused.)

"However, I'm afraid Carlon has been masturbating in his room again. We made him go for a walk, but you might want to give his knob-er, *doorknob* another wipe with an alcohol swab before you go into his room to check on him tonight."

'It's funny how these shift handovers go...' Andy reflected to himself. Often with so much emphasis on the basic bodily functions, especially in elderly and surgical settings. These are subjects which the average outsider is less-than-comfortable with. But within Nursing circles, such natural functions are of primary importance and stripped of any taboo, they become the topic of 'normal' conversation.

This is one of the main reasons why nurses and some other health professionals often have such a way-out (or maybe just more basic) concept of reality. When a person desperately needs your hand up their arse to remove ten days of painfully-impacted faeces, small talk kinda goes out of the window. There is little place for taboos in nursing, especially Psychiatric Nursing.

Andy looked down at his watch: 7:05pm. This was going to be a long shift...

Part II: Pulp Friction..

*After a few years of working at **The House**, you can only string out a handover consisting of 15 residents' daily bodily activities for so long, without diverging from the topic-at-hand. Or falling asleep...*

After a couple of minutes somebody nudged Maudlin from her spontaneous narcosis and Bettie kindly mopped up some of the drool which we had all been watching with gritted teeth, as it gradually coursed its way down the front of Maudlin's tunic.

"Has she been helping herself to the residents' medication again?" murmured Glenda, my sidekick for the coming night shift.

"She's been like that all day," said Rocky, one of the few other male RNs based at the house. "I think she's been putting in too much overtime."

But Maudlin seemed to rouse from her stupor and continued unabashed. "Oh, did you hear there was another rally on the weekend? The Wilderness Society put on a thing about that stinking Pulp Mill they're wanting to build down here. They reckon about 3000 turned up."

There was a general murmur of interest. "Yeah, good thing too," retorted Rocky, warming to his topic. "Be the worst bloody thing they could do - it'd totally fuck up the environment and we'd be drinking our own recycled piss water for the rest of our lives. I'd like to kill that bastard." There was a mumble of collective assent as Rocky wiped his projected spittle from Maudlin's forehead. "Er, sorry about that mate."

Just then Brian, one of the residents, appeared at the doorway of the Nursing Station and pushed open the upper half of the barn-style door. Sawing the door into two halves had been a great idea. That way the staff could interact with the residents without having to behold anything below the belt, such as the urine-soaked trousers which Brian stood in. "Hey Andy, you gonna help me have a shower tonight?"

"Yeah, sure Brian, no worries," Andy replied, "Just let us finish handover and I'll be with you, after supper and cigarettes, eh?"

Although he was fully-mobile and relatively self-caring, no amount of staff prompting seemed to prevent Brian from pissing in his trousers almost every day. So, the assisted showers were an important evening ritual. And Andy knew he wouldn't have to handle the malodorous strides too much; all he had to do was whistle and they'd jump into the washing machine of their own accord.

"Okay, mate." Brian tipped his urine-soaked hat (God knows how he managed to get it up there) and closed the door hatch.

The unmistakable shuffle indicated Brian had moved down the corridor, out of earshot. Rocky checked the door; one of the other residents, Grezelda, sometimes tried to listen to handover by lingering near the office. However, the advanced stench of fresh urine/faeces/general fishiness which followed her around was always a dead giveaway. "All clear."

Andy forced himself to imagine a field full of violets and focused back on the day report...

Part III: Student Nurses..

*Almost all Nursing speciality areas play host to the up-and-coming aspirants of our grand profession, the Student Nurses. The occasional student nurse rotation is generally considered to be **a good thing**, especially if the students are keen and willing to get stuck in. Naturally there are important procedures and traditional initiation rights which must be strictly adhered to...*

"The students have been a great help this shift," said Maudlin, "I let them go off duty early today as they said they had to *go to the uni library. (yes Maudlin, I'm sure that's just where they'll be...)*

"I bet." said Glenda, "So how is this this batch shaping up?"

It's funny how some staff referred to the latest semester's students as a *batch*, like they're little clones coming off some kind of standard production line or something. Andy thought back to his uni days and wondered if this mightn't be an accurate description.

"They're not bad," Maudlin replied, "We've got one male and one female this time. Jeff, the male, is interesting..."

"Yeah," interjected Rocky, "The dude's got so many studs and earrings and bits of metal shit sticking out of his face. One week here and it'll all be showing signs of advanced rust I reckon."

Earrings, especially droopy ones, are considered *a bad thing* to wear in Psychiatric settings. There have been cases of them getting ripped out. And blokes with tongue studs only meant one thing in Andy's book. None of this was an appropriate or effective way to try and gain a patient's confidence. Unless you - oh never mind...

Jeff clearly had a number of unresolved personal issues and possibly a diagnosable Personality Disorder, all of which meant of course, that he would be perfectly suited to being some kind of Mental Health Professional.

"The girl, Jenny, she's pretty good though," continued Maudlin, "She doesn't seem to mind getting her hands dirty."

Everyone nodded their approval. Not minding getting your hands dirty was considered *a good thing*. And just as well, working at *The House*. Everyone knew what Maudlin meant. Since the shift from hospital-based Schools of Nursing to university training, the expectations of some student nurses had also apparently shifted. The amount of clinical exposure had been greatly reduced since the universities took over and some students certainly did not take kindly to some of the more hands-on (or *hands-in*) aspects of Nursing.
During the early years of university-based nurse training, some of the more experienced hospital-trained RNs had resented this new breed of nurses emerging onto the scene. Others welcomed the more academic focus. Having trained originally in the hospital system and then at university-based Nursing studies, Andy could see both sides of the argument. Another trend was that fewer males were entering the profession and

fewer still wanted to go into Psychiatry after they graduated.

And it was true that some of the fun and well, frolics had disappeared from the workplace. Andy thought back to his own training days...

Part IV: Initiation...

Sitting in the staff room on a hot Summer's evening shift. No air conditioning at *The House*. The foetid miasma from the local abattoir wafted hotly in through the open window, competing with the local stench of residential bodily emanations and cheap microwaved lasagne. Andy drifted in and out of consciousness. Risking brain damage, he kept his nose out the window and found himself drifting back 20 years and to thoughts of cooler climes...

It was 1984, a significant time for classic sci-fi fans. However instead of George Orwell and a doublethink culture, we had Boy George and Culture Club. No-one saw that one coming. Doubleplusgood indeed...

On his 21st birthday Andy had made the switch from being a cheeky, spotty young suit working in a bank in England, to a cheeky, spotty young student nurse with a shiny, new career of helping people with severe mental health problems. As he entered the Broadland School of Nursing that Winter, he reflected that it might not be all that different. The pressures in the world of Banking could be brutal - especially for those higher up, but Andy knew he wasn't destined for the fiscal echelons. Interestingly at his level, the pay was the same...

The second nursing school clinical placement was Psychogeriatrics (as it was known then) - not a place for the faint-hearted or the nasally sensitive. Andy was currently *enjoying* one of the traditional welcoming rituals of the ward, from outside the ward. Actually, from outside one of the windows of the ward. To be more exact, from the inside of a soaking wet laundry bag which was suspended from the ledge of said window.

"We'll haul you up in ten minutes..." the deep Wurzelly (as in Gummidge) voice of the burly Charge Nurse boomed out of the window, "That's if you don't manage to escape all on your own. Or fall..." he added with a snigger. Big Ivan was the Wurzels nurse-in-charge and Andy had been no match at the hands of Ivan-The-Terrible and his equally wrestler-esque Nursing Assistant, Marauding Mike.

The laundry bag creaked a bit at the seams as the rope tying it to a radiator inside gave a little; but it held strong. Andy shivered from the bath (fully clothed of course) he had received prior to being stuffed into the bag, carried up the stairs and rolled out the window ledge. Apparently, the exercise was a *Test Of Character*. A 'survive or die' kind of thing. If you passed, you were in (and presumably cured of any latent claustrophobic, hydrophobic and acrophobic tendencies in the process). Efficient and cost-effective. Nothing like a bit of 'Implosion Therapy' to start the day...

Andy reflected on his time on the ward as his laundry bag gently swayed in the breeze. By its very nature the work was very, well *manual* as only a fully-occupied twenty-five bed psychogeriatric ward with an incontinence rate of 85% can be. Lots of mouths to feed, arses to polish and piss to squeegee.

Naturally a clean set of overalls was essential and Andy had already suffered the ignominy of arriving at work and donning his white nurse's coat, only to find the arm sleeves sewn up or the pockets full of wet talcum powder or the buttons all cut off. And being tied to a wheelchair for a speedy blindfolded two-wheeled 'ride of death' through the wards had been an unspeakable thrill which left one lost for words.

The bag lurched, pulling Andy from his reverie. He thought he heard the sounds of muffled sniggers above and then the rope gave way and the laundry bag plummeted...

...about twelve inches and landed on the grass.

Andy fought against the severed bag ties and jumped out. As the bag fell from around him, he stood and found himself face-to-face with the window and the grins of Big Ivan and Mike beaming back at him. The "let's get you up the stairs" bit had been a bluff and he was still on the ground floor.

The lesson-for-the-day: This is what it's like to shit your pants. Remember how it feels, when you're wiping someone's arse. A brutal if memorable lesson in humility and empathy...

(Ah, so it had all been a *lesson*; a carefully constructed pedagogy. What fun! Funny however, how words like *sadistic* and *psychopaths* and *f**king* tended   to spring to mind...)

Part V: Evening Shift..

Evenings at The House are usually pretty quiet affairs. There's the supper round, the medication round and the cigarette round to organise. Not necessarily in that order. Most people smoke, most are on medication, most are a bit overweight. Often the three are intertwined. But generally, evenings are pretty low-key and relaxed...

"I'm gonna kill you, you f*cking old c*nt!" the yell came from the residents' kitchen, the voice - the unmistakable falsetto of Jamie, the youngest and newest resident at *The House*. In the Nurses' Office, Andy looked up from his microwaved lasagne and carefully wiped his lips with a napkin, "I'll deal with this one."

One doesn't spend twenty years in Nursing only to panic at the mere sound of murder and mayhem. Nor blanch at choice expletives. Emotion is a funny thing. Some people are very in tune with their feelings, others not so. The trick here is not to wade into such a situation showing too much excitement yourself as this can heighten the levels of arousal.

The scene in the kitchen was a picture indeed. Brian was rolling on the floor, thrashing against another of the older residents, Eddie. Eddie in turn, was attempting to strangle Brian. And just to add colour, Jamie was yelling at Brian at the top of his voice and trying to kick him on the floor.

Andy calmly moved in and asked Jamie to stand back a few paces so he could get to the two blokes brawling on the floor. Both the combatants were elderly and rather unfit and they could almost have been locked in an amorous embrace, sweating and grunting and swearing away at each other. Andy tried hard not to smile.

With the help of Glenda, the other RN, they physically prised the two aspiring gladiators apart and calmed them down in separate corners of the room. Definitely a two-person job, breaking up fights. It's also important to get the combatants talking, expressing themselves verbally, getting the anger out without resorting to more physical aggression. There was a bit more shouting as Brian and Eddie faced off across the dining room, but the situation gradually calmed to a grumble.

Andy and Glenda took some time making sure the other residents were OK and the unit gradually returned back to normality again (and don't get me started on what's *normal*).
The incident had occurred due to Brian's tendency to guzzle half the milk from the communal jug. Usually, the residents report such things and the staff have a quiet word with the offender. Serious fights in mental health institutions are comparatively rare, although the tensions of any group of people living together are bound to result in minor clashes from time to time.

The nurses returned to their office to finish tea. "Did you see that gardening show on TV last night...?" asked Glenda, sipping her coffee.

"Nah, I never watch the telly," Andy was back, happily munching on his luke-warm lasagne, "Real life's enough excitement for me..."

Part VI: Rehab and Reality...

Rehabilitation generally refers to helping an individual learn or regain those skills required for more independent living. In Mental Health it is a process of working with people to help them regain control of their lives which psychiatric illness (and sometimes institutionalisation), has taken away.

Andy knew a lot about de-institutionalisation. It had been *the* buzzword when he had trained in the 1980s. At nine syllables long it was one of the longest words he knew. And he also knew you'd be counting them out on your fingers as he completed the end of the sentence. See...nine.

The eighties had been a time of revolution in psychiatric - sorry, *Mental Health* care. The language was changing, the asylums were closing and erstwhile patients were being discharged into community care and this was considered ***a very good thing***.

Any mental health nursing student worth his or her salt disparaged long-term psychiatric inpatient care and any psychiatric luddites (read: *backwater* staff) who dared to ever support it. We loudly championed ***deinstitutionalisation!*** throughout our assignments. Just as three decades later any self-respecting student would ferociously ejaculate the mantra of the *new* **Recovery Model**, whilst scrutinising seasoned clinicians for any signs of dissension from The New Order.

Andy mused that the streets were once again awash with babies and bathwater...

In theory the idea of getting people out of the psychiatric hospitals and into environments promoting choice and freedom had been a decent one. For centuries people had been labelled as 'mad' and 'insane' and locked away from society's gaze (out of eye, out-of-mind) in distant institutions. Now it was time to return them to the loving communities from whence they came, who would of course embrace then with open arms...

And Random House was one such place. An environment where the previously incarcerated would be able to learn to reintegrate into polite society, to shop, get haircuts, drink beer and wank openly. Except of course the people - the locals - didn't want them there for some reason. It had been a time of fine hypocrisies indeed. A time of "Yes, these people should be back in the community where they belong" but "I don't want them near me."

Andy and his kind had fought the good fight to get people with mental illness accepted into the community. An important stock-in-trade part of the job had been to advocate for the cause. Of course, he mused, there were *client advocates* to do that now...
"Hey cheer up Nurse Andy!" said a bright apparition standing at the office door. "Wot you got to be so down in the dumps about?"

Andy looked up at Catty, a lifelong Bipolar (amongst other things) sufferer whom he had looked after on-and-off for nearly twenty years. Catty grinned back maniacally through a mask of Max Factor's finest.

"Come and give us a hug Andy Pandy! I heard you was on tonight. You doin' the night shift again...? We've got sandwiches for supper tonight and I've been cleaning my room up with the day staff. Come and have a look..."

Snapped from his reverie, Andy got up and returned the hug, "It's good to see you too..."

You can take the person out of the institution...

Part VII: Body Fluids..

Most nurses are intimately acquainted with the various aqueous contents that the human organism is capable of producing. And the various human organisms living at *Random House* were quite adept at spraying their assorted fluids around the place.

Urine

An obvious start and *the* most popular fluid by far. Perhaps surprisingly, it was most frequently encountered in toilets, which were themselves most frequently encountered in the un-flushed state. But this was *a good thing*. We were very happy to find urine in the toilet. Mainly because of all the other places we also encountered it.

The floor was the second most popular location and the cause of many a nocturnal skid: if the stench didn't get you then the resulting head injury would usually finish the job. Those with waterproof soles remained relatively safe and dry-of-foot; not so for the semi-comatose night nurse, warily staggering out for a wee in stockinged feet.

The mop and bucket never, ever got put into the broom cupboard, but lived permanently in the toilet area; there was no sluice room. Following the morning cleaner's visit, as the heat of the day wore on, the corridor past the nurses' station would become stickier and stickier and your shoes would make that *schtick schtick* noise as you walked along. I used to think they should take the flooring from *The House* and stick it around the walls of the International Space Station, thus permitting astronauts to stride around with confidence in zero gravity...

The final popular locations for stray traces of urine were on people's hands, down the front of trousers (mostly residents) and splashed on shoes (mostly night staff). One quickly learned not to shake hands with people.

Snot

Now, I truly tried hard to find a nicer term here, but *nasal mucus* doesn't really begin to describe what we were sometimes forced to look at wobbling around, whilst holding a conversation with one particular resident, especially in the Winter months. Avoiding the strategically-placed tissue box and verbal prompts to let us have our tea in peace, he would lean on the lower barn door watching us eating our evening meal. We would stare back, watching him watching us, our eyes trying not to follow the stream of snot as it dripped down his jumper, the snail-trail eventually coalescing with some other substance apparently on the way up. I rarely eat lasagne any more...

Blood

Like nostrils, tempers were known to flare from time to time, but it was part testament to the place that there was very little bloodshed. On a regular basis. Which wasn't part of a normal process.

We did have a resident with diabetes who during a psychotic episode, decided that the needle in the test kit was less than efficient. So, he used his t-rusty penknife to open a deep wound in his finger. He was relieved to discover his blood sugar level (BSL) was within normal ranges, although he almost amputated his digit and locked up his jaws in the pursuit of scientific discovery.

Diarrhoea

This tale wouldn't be complete without reference to the delivered hospital food. What they termed 'quick-chill' we called quick *kill* and there was a theory going around that this was used to keep the residential population rotated through. Rotated through *what* I never found out, but I suspect they meant the lavatories.

Although fruit was readily available, the mushy meals and lack of willingness to exercise (despite our efforts) didn't feature well when it came to healthy stool production. I wouldn't say things were bad but we were on first name terms with the local plumber and invited him to most functions.

Sperm (yes, indeed)

Although thankfully rarely encountered in its natural state, the proliferation of human spermatozoa was nevertheless a concern, especially for the more genteel members of staff. Generally, the problem was isolated to the occasional shirt front (usually residents'). However, the door handle to one particular side room regularly rewarded the unwary staff member (or unprepared visitor) with a certain stickiness of hand and downturn of spirit.

One innovative person did try screwing a latex glove dispenser to the wall nearby. However, the ensuing consumption of its contents mysteriously skyrocketed out of proportion with staff usage patterns, leading to an increase in clinical costs.

Talk about *blowing the budget...*

Psychosurgery

Psychosurgery is generally considered to be a form of surgery which was performed on a person's brain to treat severe cases of mental illness. Frontal Lobotomy is a surgical procedure severing the connection between the prefrontal cortex and the rest of the brain.

The frontal lobe of the brain controls a number of advanced cognitive functions, as well as motor control. Motor control is located at the rear of the frontal lobe, and is usually unaffected by psychosurgery. The anterior or prefrontal area is involved in impulse control, judgement with everyday life and situations, language, memory, motor function, problem solving, sexual behaviour, socialization and spontaneity. Frontal lobes assist in planning, coordinating, controlling and executing behaviour.

How and Why

One of the theories behind psychosurgery was that these nerves were somehow malformed or damaged, and if they were severed, they might regenerate into new, healthy connections. The main indications for psychosurgery included severe chronic anxiety, depression with risk of suicide, incapacitating obsessive-compulsive disorder and high levels of aggression. However, contrary to popular belief, the operation was not only used on psychiatric patients. Many people were lobotomized for intractable pain, such as chronic, severe backaches or agonizing headaches.

Registered Nurses were often assigned to *special* the lobotomy patients during the initial 48 hours after surgery. As soon as possible, the patients were returned to their own ward. Staff then had to feed, bathe and dress these patients, as considerable time was needed to re-educate a lobotomy patient to care for himself.

The three most popular types of psychosurgery were prefrontal leucotomy, prefrontal lobotomy and transorbital lobotomy.

The *leucotomy* (developed by Portuguese surgeon Egas Moniz) basically involved drilling holes in the skull in order to access the brain. Once visible, the surgeon would sever the nerves using a pencil-sized tool called a leucotome. It had a slide mechanism on the side that would deploy a wire loop or loops from the tip. The idea was to be able to slide the pencil into the pre-drilled holes in the top of skull, into the brain, then use the slide to make the loop(s) come out. The surgeon could sever the nerves by removing cores of brain tissue, slide the loop back in, and the operation was complete.

A *lobotomy* also utilized drilled holes, but in the upper forehead instead of the top of the skull. It was also different in that the surgeon used a blade to cut the brain instead of a leucotome.

The infamous *transorbital lobotomy* was a blind operation, in that the surgeon did not know for certain if he had severed the nerves or not. A sharp chisel-like object would be inserted through the eye socket between the upper lid and eye. When the doctor thought he was at about the right spot, he would hit the end of the instrument with a hammer.

Also known as the "ice pick lobotomy", this unpleasant procedure was developed and made particularly popular in the U.S. by one Walter Freeman. Freeman literally used an ice pick and rubber mallet to perform his fine work. In what is widely considered to be a highly invasive procedure, Freeman would hammer the ice pick into the skull just above the tear duct and wiggle it around.

Throughout 1930-1950 Freeman purportedly travelled around in a van, (which he called his "lobotomobile"), demonstrating the procedure in many medical centers. Leaving no visible scars, the ice pick lobotomy was hailed as a great advance in "minimally invasive" surgery, with some operations performed reportedly using only local anaesthesia.

Freeman's advocacy led to great popularity for lobotomy as a general cure for all perceived ills, including misbehaviour in children. Up to 50,000 patients may have been lobotomised during this time.

Benefits

It is possible that some patients did benefit from the later forms of psychosurgery. What were considered 'good' results at the time often came down to changes in personality and reduced spontaneity, including making the person quieter and decreasing their libido. Some forms of schizophrenia may have responded favourably, where there were theories regarding frontal lobe involvement.

However, certain types of inappropriate behaviours increased from the resulting lowered impulse control.

The surgery also often decreased one's ability to function as a member of the community, through a diminishing of problem-solving skills and reductions in flexibility and adaptiveness.

Interestingly the operations seemed to have no bearing on IQ, except with respect to problem solving.

There was a strong division amongst the medical profession as to the viability of the treatment and also concern over the irreversible nature of the operation. There was also concern regarding the appropriateness of extending the seemed surgery into the treatment of unsuitable cases, such as drug and alcohol dependence and sexual disorders.

By the 1960s, the number of operations was in decline as the procedure became much less fashionable.

Improvements in psychopharmacology and behaviour therapy gave the opportunity for more effective and less-invasive treatment.

The era of lobotomy is now generally regarded as a somewhat *barbaric* episode in psychiatric history.
Most of this article is true...

"I see dead people...everywhere."

He lives somewhere on the island of Tasmania and he shuns a lot of publicity, so we shall call him Claus. This is to respect both the man himself and the former identities of his work companions. When they walked amongst the living.

Claus works for an agency, some branches of which have great need of his unusual skills. His workplace is a medium-sized studio which is full of stuffed animals, dinosaur replicas and rather unnerving examples of his other speciality.

It's a bit like walking into the back of a SAW II film set, which is not so strange as Claus does some work for the film industry too. He tells me he has a few ah, private customers whom he helps to indulge their unorthodox taste, grooving on Thanatos and all that. Just animals of course; nothing too weird.

A couple of wild cats stare out at me from behind the window of the freeze-dryer unit as we talk. One has even got a rat in its mouth, preserving the relationship of hunter and hunted beyond death. Do we have wildcats in Tasmania? Well, there are two less now. Or maybe Aunt Maudlin just wanted Tiddles immortalised as a coffee-table conversation piece. The grandchildren will love it. More tea, Vicar...?

Some wag or other has probably already passed the phrase about taxidermy being a dying art, but I prefer not to be so obvious. Not that Claus doesn't have a sense of humour, no. Quite the opposite. There's nothing Claus likes more than to take the odd invited but unsuspecting visitor on a tour of his studio and seeing how long it takes them to pass out or throw up.

I suppose that's a black sense of humour really isn't it. But it's totally appropriate - given the macabre nature of this man's work. Because he doesn't just *do* animals... You see,
Claus chops real people up into little pieces.

And there it is. The table. A table with the white sheet over it. Slightly familiar ripples in the cloth hint at what might lie below. Suddenly I'm not sure if I want to see what lies below. But the sheet is sliding away.

I'm certainly no stranger to death, having witnessed both self-violence and suicidal injury under the most extreme circumstances. However, the sight of the dismembered bodies reminded me less of a *post mortem* than of a large butcher's workbench. Except the limbs, torsos and heads were human. A cannibal's smorgasbord, as it were.

Claus's particular claim-to-fame in certain circles, is his technique of preserving the body parts by sealing them with a secret recipe of chemicals, thus preventing the natural decay of the tissues. Claus calls his technique *plasticisation*.
Certainly, on picking a sample up, the skin and soft tissues feel hard to the touch. However, no plastic model could be this accurate in its depiction of the skeletal form, the musculature, the blood vessels. Even parts such as eyelashes and pubic hair remain intact, frozen in time.

Naturally such a fine resource is extremely valuable to anyone who needs to study the minutiae of the human anatomy, such as students of the healing sciences. And of course, the cadavers themselves had legally donated their bodies to the cause while still in life

No need for Egor anymore, but Frankenstein will always need his raw material...

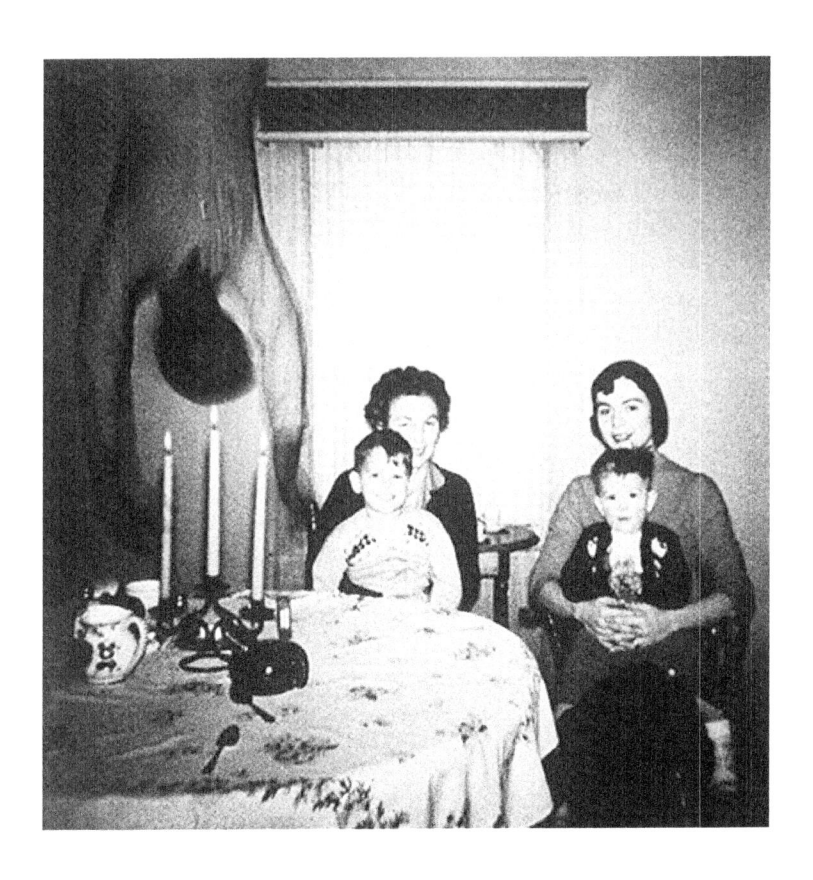

Gallows Humour

Mental illness is not a laughing matter, but it can have its moments. Often it helps to maintain perspective by seeing the funny side of situations and sometimes laughter really is the best medicine...

During a visit to the mental asylum, a visitor asked the Director what the criterion was which defined whether or not a patient should be institutionalised.

"Well," said the Director, "We fill up a bathtub, then we offer a teaspoon, a teacup and a bucket to the patient and ask him or her to empty the bathtub."

"Oh, I understand," said the visitor, "A normal person would use the bucket because it's bigger than the spoon or the teacup."

"No." said the Director, "A normal person would pull the plug. Do you want a bed near the window?"

The senior nurses and doctors in a lunatic asylum have a meeting and decide that one of their patients may be potentially well enough for discharge. So, they decide to test him and take him to the movies.

When they get to the movie theatre, there are 'wet paint' signs pointing to the benches. The nurses and doctors just sit down, but the patient puts a newspaper down first and then sits down.

The staff get all excited because they think he may be in touch with reality now. So, they ask him, "Why did you put the newspaper down first?"

He answers, "So I'd be higher and have a better view."

After hearing that one of the patients in the mental asylum had saved another from a suicide attempt by pulling him out of the bathtub, the asylum director called him to his office...

Director: Mr Bush, your records and your heroic behaviour indicate that you are ready to go home. I'm only sorry that the man you saved, later killed himself with a rope around his neck!

Mr Bush: Oh, he didn't kill himself. I hung him up to dry.

A bloke is walking past a high, solid wooden fence at the local lunatic asylum when he hears all the residents inside chanting, "Thirteen! Thirteen! Thirteen!"

He continues walking along the long fence but, being a curious person, he can't help wonder why they are chanting "Thirteen!" over and over. Could it be that they are chugging beer? Are they perhaps taking turns beating one of the inmates? Maybe they are counting the number of patients that have leapt off of the roof thus far.

His curiosity peaks and he frantically searches for a hole in the fence so that he may see what is going on. Finally, he spots one a few feet ahead. The hole is low in the fence and he has to kneel down to peer inside.

He moves into position and peeks into the hole. As he looks in, someone inside pokes him in the eye! Then everyone inside the asylum starts chanting, "Fourteen! Fourteen! Fourteen!"

The doctor was on his daily round of the mental asylum and had just entered the room of two of his long-term patients. One was sawing imaginary wood into hundreds of pieces and the other was hanging upside down from the ceiling.

"What are you doing?" the doctor asked the first man.

"I'm sawing wood," he said, "Isn't that obvious?"

"Well, what's your friend doing?"

"Oh, don't mind him, he thinks he's a lightbulb."

"Don't you think you should help him down before all the blood rushes to his head?" continued the doctor.

"What!?" exclaimed the man, "And work in the bloody dark!?"

A man went to a psychiatrist for his phobia.

"Doctor," he said, "I've got trouble. Every time I get into bed, I think there's somebody under it. I get under the bed; I think there's somebody on top of it. Top, under, top, under. You gotta help me, I'm going mad!"

"Just put yourself in my hands for two years," said the shrink, "Come to me three times a week, and I'll cure your fears."

"How much do you charge?"

"A hundred pounds per visit."

"I'll sleep on it," said the man.

Six months later the doctor met the man on the street.

"Why didn't you ever come to see me again?" asked the psychiatrist.

"For a hundred quid a visit? A bartender cured me for ten pounds."

"Is that so! How?"

"He told me to cut the legs off the bed!"

Neurotics build castles in the sky
Psychotics live in them
Psychiatrists collect the rent

Two elderly couples were enjoying friendly conversation when one of the men asked the other, "Fred, how was the memory clinic you went to last month?"

"Outstanding," Fred replied. "They taught us all the latest psychological techniques - visualization, association - it made a huge difference for me."

"That's great! What was the name of the clinic?"

Fred went blank. He thought and thought, but couldn't remember. Then a smile broke across his face and he asked, "What do you call that red flower with the long stem and thorns?"

"You mean a rose?"

"Yes, that's it!" He turned to his wife, "Rose, what was the name of that clinic?"

Patient: Doctor, my wife thinks I'm crazy because I like sausages.
Psychiatrist: Nonsense! I like sausages too.
Patient: Good, you should come and see my collection. I've got hundreds of them.

Patient: Doctor, you must help me. I'm under such a lot of stress, I keep losing my temper with people.
Doctor: Tell me about your problem.
Patient: I JUST DID, DIDN'T I, YOU STUPID BASTARD!!!

A man is strolling past the mental hospital and suddenly remembers an important meeting.

Unfortunately, his watch has stopped and he cannot tell if he is late or not. Then, he notices a patient similarly strolling about within the hospital fence.

Calling out to the patient, the man says, "Pardon me, sir, but do you have the time?"

The patient calls back, "One moment!" and throws himself upon the ground, pulling out a short stick as he does. He pushes the stick into the ground, and, pulling out a carpenter's level, assures himself that the stick is vertical.

With a compass, the patient locates north and with a steel ruler, measures the precise length of the shadow cast by the stick.

Withdrawing a slide rule from his pocket, the patient calculates rapidly, then swiftly packs up all his tools and turns back to the pedestrian, saying, "It is now precisely 3:29 pm, provided today is August 16th, which I believe it is."

The man can't help but be impressed by this demonstration, and sets his watch accordingly.

Before he leaves, he says to the patient, "That was really quite remarkable, but tell me, what do you do on a cloudy day, or at night, when the stick casts no shadow?" The patient holds up his wrist and says, "I suppose I'd just look at my watch."

A man phones a mental hospital and asks the receptionist if there is anybody in Room 27.

She goes and checks, and comes back to the phone, telling him that the room is empty.

"Good," says the man. "That means I must have really escaped...!"

Andrew Mallett - a potted history

Starting hospital-based training in Norwich, England in the Winter of 1984, I emerged as a Registered Mental Nurse three years later. I even had a white coat. These years saw the gradual abandonment of the big former 'lunatic asylums' and the celebration of *deinstitutionalisation* - the buzz word of the zeitgeist. All good in theory but many former inpatients effectively ended up on the streets, vulnerable and untreated.
The lovely old buildings themselves often got squashed, reused for offices or sold off as flats. This was true for both the UK and Australia, the latter with many beautiful old asylums being built from sandstone.

Based at Hellesdon Hospital, Norwich, I also did tours of duty at Thorpe St. Andrews Hospital, The David Rice Hospital, The Norvic (Forensic) Clinic and did time in Norwich Prison who were keen to recruit. On the good side. Mostly.

A trip to Australia in 1989 found me working in a private mental health unit, Sydney's eminent Northside Clinic. I'd shipped my beloved Suzuki GS(X)1200 'drag bike' ahead and proceeded to fang it around Highway 1 on a work visa. I ended up in Townsville working as a Community Psych Nurse.

A subsequent thrash down to Tasmania the following year secured a bid for Australian Residency. I worked in an acute psychiatric unit and later moved on to running a day centre for the long term mentally ill. With nurse training in Australia shifting to the university sector it was time to upgrade the qual's which involved returning to NSW in 1993 to undertake a Nursing degree at Sydney's University of Technology.

After graduating I travelled and taught English, facilitated by a TEFLA Certificate at the Bondhi Junction School of English. By that time, I had returned to Sydney's Northside Clinic and presently took a position there as Nurse Unit Manager. Sometime later Redfern Community Mental Health Services beckoned, leading to a return to the community and a Graduate Diploma in Psychotherapy followed.

A growing interest in computers caused a move to the celebrated Rozelle (Psychiatric) Hospital to help develop an IT infrastructure for various hospitals and health centres around central Sydney. After spending some time travelling between Australia, the UK and Greece, I took a position as a Team Leader at Compaq Computers in Western Sydney in 1999. Our team's tasks included developing and supplying computer systems to Australian forces serving in East Timor. The systems had to be robust enough to be run from a generator in the middle of a field.

A return to the beautiful roads and countryside of Van Diemen's Land in 2000 led to more two-wheeled tarmac thrashing and a teaching position with TAFE Tasmania. This provided opportunities to gain more certification in both the IT and VET (Vocational Education & Training) fields. I later transferred to TAFE's health programme, shifting from teaching IT to teaching Nursing.

This background was about to lead to an unexpected opportunity in 2008. While undertaking a Master's Degree in Clinical Nursing at the University of Tasmania, I was invited to join the Faculty of Health. Utas needed someone with clinical and IT skills to develop their new Simulation Centre, used for training nursing and medical students and post-grad stuff.

Closely resembling a real acute clinical facility combined with a sound studio, the centre housed a number of 'Sim People' - simulated humans on whom clinicians could practise their skills at resuscitation and other interventions. It was a time of developing cutting-edge training facilities at campuses in Tasmania and Sydney (popping back to Rozelle Hospital again) and I also lectured in med/surg/psych Nursing at the Tassie campus.

Despite a love of teaching, I decided I wasn't an academic and began hankering for a return to life at the coalface. So, 2010 saw a return to clinical work with the community mental health teams and later with the Medicare-funded Mental Health Nurse Incentive Programme. This involved working in primary mental health, taking GP referrals for patients requiring psychotherapy and treatment for more severe forms of mental illness.

Subsequent positions have included phlebotomy RN at the Australian Red Cross Blood Service and Court Liaison Officer with Community Forensic Mental Health.

I do look back on my years in the erstwhile asylums with fondness. There was a real family atmosphere and some incredible times were had. Living-in at the **nurses'**

home was a complete riot! I saw things that made me laugh. I saw things that made me sad. Maybe one day we'll all go back to the days of yore and institutional care, once more. There are so many ways in which people were better off...

Andy Mallett

Printed in Great Britain
by Amazon